Let's dive into the world of camera apps on F-Droid. Finding the absolute "best" one depends on your specific needs and preferences. Here's a lineup of some top contenders, each bringing its own strengths to the table:

For those who love control:
Open Camera:

Open Camera

Camera App

A feature rich camera application, including:

* auto-stabilise option
* multitouch zoom
* flash/torch
* choice of focus modes
* face detection
* front/back camera support
* change recording resolution
* video/audio recording
* timer
* burst mode
* silenceable shutter
* configurable gui
* geotagging
* external microphone support

Author: Mark Harman — License: GNU General Public License v3.0 or later — Website — Issue Tracker — Source Code — Changelog — Build Metadata

 This open-source gem is packed with features and perfect for advanced users. It lets you take charge with manual controls for white balance, ISO, exposure, and focus. Plus, it throws in burst mode, scene modes, and HDR for good measure.

For simplicity and privacy advocates:

Simple Camera

Quick photo and video camera with a flash, customizable aspect ratio

Simple Camera: If you prefer a lightweight and user-friendly experience, Simple Camera is your go-to. It keeps it essential with features like focus, timer, and flash, all while maintaining a no-ads and no-unnecessary-permissions policy.

For capturing those specific moments:

Libre Camera

Modern camera app to take pictures and record videos

Libre Camera is a free and open source camera app to take pictures and record videos written in Flutter and Dart.

Libre Camera: Sporting a modern interface, Libre Camera is your companion for everyday photography and quick captures. With a timer, burst mode, and focus control, it's got everything you need.

For unleashing your inner artist:

ObscuraCam: The Privacy Camera

Picture anonymity: Take pictures & blur identities with this privacy camera app

Obscura Camera: Get ready for a vintage-style experience! Obscura Camera brings analog film simulations, light leaks, and double exposure to the table for those who want to get creative with their photography.

Remember, the best way to find your perfect F-Droid camera app is to explore and give a few a try based on your needs. Reading reviews and checking out screenshots can also help you get a better sense of what each app brings to the table. Happy snapping!

Hey there, tech newcomers! Let me introduce you to F-Droid, a cool app store and software repository for Android. Think of it as an alternative to the Google Play Store, but with a twist – it exclusively hosts free and open-source software (FOSS). Now, let's break down what makes F-Droid stand out:

What it brings to the table:

1. **Open-source apps:** This means that the source code of the apps is open for anyone to check out and tweak. It's like having a backstage pass to your apps, offering more transparency and security compared to closed-source alternatives.

2. **No ads or tracking:** F-Droid apps usually skip the annoying ads and user tracking tools. Great news for those who value their privacy!

3. **Diverse app selection:** Even though F-Droid is all about FOSS, it still packs a punch with a wide array of apps. From social media and messaging to games and productivity tools, you'll find a bit of everything.

4. **User-friendly interface:** Access F-Droid through a website or grab the app client for your Android device. Either way, the interfaces are designed to be beginner-friendly – no tech wizardry required.

5. **Independent from Google:** Unlike the Play Store, F-Droid isn't under Google's thumb. This gives it the freedom to host apps that might not meet Google's strict policies.

Things to keep in mind:

1. **App selection:** While F-Droid has a solid library, it might not have all the latest or trendiest apps you're used to seeing on the Play Store.

2. **Updates:** Updates on F-Droid might not be as speedy as on the Play Store since they depend on volunteers. So, be patient!

3. **Security:** F-Droid apps go through basic security checks, but it's always wise to check reviews before hitting that install button.

In a nutshell, F-Droid is a fantastic choice for those who prioritize privacy, transparency, and open-source software. It's a reliable way to discover and install a bunch of FOSS apps for your Android device. If you're curious to learn more, check out their website: https://f-droid.org/en/

dandelion*

diaspora* social network client

A client for the community-run, distributed social network diaspora*.
It adds useful features to your networking experience:

- Quick access to most diaspora* features
- Customize everything to own preferences
- Share content from and to the app
- Proxy support (Tor/Orbot supported)
- In-app-browser to view articles
- Dark/AMOLED mode available
- Available in many languages
- Browse tags and aspects

Use in any language that the app is translated in - for example in German but have English as system language.

Looking for a pod to register? The app lists many pods with more being listed at podupti.me.

Multiple accounts: You can use dandelion* and dandelior* to use two accounts at the same time on one device. They use a different icon and other default colors.

Notice: The app uses the Android WebView component to display contents of diaspora* pods in the mobile view. For missing features and bugs in mobile view, ask at diaspora* bugtracker.

Diaspora: A federated network for sharing text, photos, and videos, with a strong focus on privacy and decentralized control.

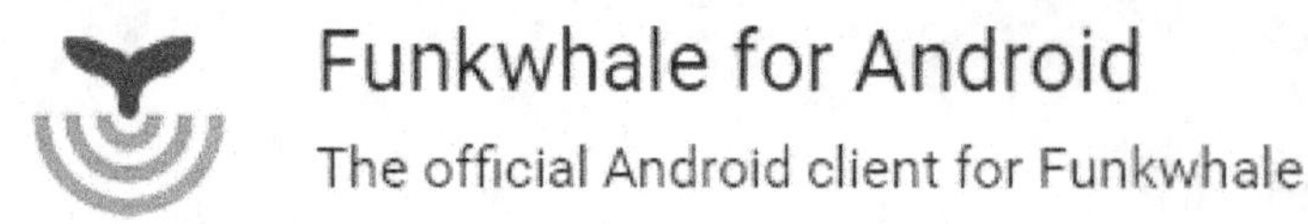

Funkwhale for Android

The official Android client for Funkwhale

Funkwhale for Android™ is an Android client for Funkwhale, a music streaming server that you can self-host. It uses Funkwhale's native API instead of the subsonic API.

This app requires an account on a Funkwhale instance to work.

You can get support or take a part in Funkwhale's development by visiting our Gitlab project. You can also join us on Matrix.

Source code : https://dev.funkwhale.audio/funkwhale/funkwhale-android
Matrix room: https://matrix.to/#/#funkwhale-android:matrix.org
Funkwhale : https://funkwhale.audio

Author: The Funkwhale Collective — **License:** MIT License — Website — Issue Tracker — Translation — Source Code — Changelog — Build Metadata

Funkwhale: For music enthusiasts, this self-hosted music streaming platform resembles SoundCloud, prioritizing user privacy and adhering to open standards.

Niche Communities and Interests:

Mobilizon

Mobilizon is a tool to help manage your events, your profiles and your groups.

Mobilizon: Dive into this event management platform designed for organizing and joining offline events within specific communities.

Manyverse

A social network off the grid

Manyverse is a social network app using the SSB protocol (Secure Scuttlebutt) where you can write posts and share with friends nearby or over the internet. It's different from mainstream social networks because your data is yours, it lives on your phone, not in the cloud. So there is no login, no company holding your data, no ads, no tracking of your activity, it's just you and your friends! The app is free and open source software, and it will always remain free.

Let's venture into the world of games on F-Droid. Pinpointing the absolute "best" is subjective, but here are some standout contenders highly regarded for their excellence in various aspects:

For the strategic minds and roguelike fans:

Shattered Pixel Dungeon

A roguelike game based on Pixel Dungeon

Shattered Pixel Dungeon: Dive into a polished dungeon crawler offering deep gameplay, challenging mechanics, and permanent death for endless replayability.

Andor's Trail

Quest-driven RPG

Quest-driven Roguelike fantasy dungeon crawler RPG with a powerful story. Uncover the truths about your home village and the disappearance of your brother.

Battle fierce monsters, gain experience and levels. Solve quests, find hidden treasures and improve your equipment.

Please note that this is a work in progress, which means that all maps are not yet done. This is mainly a version for bug-hunting and compatibility testing. Please give feedback on the project page.

Some of the content and graphics are released under non-free licenses: see GitHub page.

Anti-Features

This app has features you may not like. Learn more!

 This app contains non-free assets

Andor's Trail: Embark on a turn-based strategy adventure featuring beautiful pixel art, deep tactical combat, and an engaging campaign with multiple branching paths.

OpenTTD

A simulation game based on the popular game "Transport Tycoon Deluxe"

NOTE: This is a fork of https://github.com/pelya/openttd-android since development there is on hold currently.

OpenTTD: Manage your transportation empire in this classic transport tycoon game with open-source development, expansive features, and limitless possibilities.

For the casual and puzzle enthusiasts:

2048 (Privacy Friendly)

Try to reach 2048 in this puzzle game

The application Privacy Friendly 2048 is an exciting puzzle game. The game is considered to be won if you reach the number 2048 by sliding the same numbers together. The statistic function is also part of the app. This makes it possible to get information about for example the required number of swipes and the highest achieved number of points. The Privacy Friendly 2048 has four different game modes. The app belongs to the Privacy Friendly Apps group developed by the research group SECUSO at Karlsruhe Institute of Technology.

2048: Get addicted to this tile-matching game with a simple yet challenging premise, perfect for quick bursts of gameplay.

Freebloks

Strategy board game similar to the famous board game Blokus.

This is the Android version of Freebloks 3D, an implementation of the famous board game Blokus. Try to place as many tiles on the board as possible, keeping in mind only two simple rules: your tiles must touch a corner of one of your previously placed tiles, but they must not share an edge. Can you play more tiles than your opponents?

RULES
Each player has 21 Tetris-like tiles: 12 tiles with 5 squares, 5 tiles with 4 squares, 2 tiles with 3 squares, 1 tile with 2 squares and 1 tile with 1 square.
Players take turns in placing one tile onto the 20x20 board. The first tile for each player has to be placed in their corner of the board. Each following tile has to touch a corner of one of your previous tiles, but it must never share an edge. It may share edges with the opponents' tiles though.
If a player has no more possible move, they have to pass. The game is over when no player can place a tile.
For each player, the squares of all their tiles on the board are added up. The player with the most points wins.

Freebloks: Immerse yourself in a Tetris-inspired block puzzle game with innovative mechanics, multiple game modes, and a relaxing atmosphere.

Pixel Dungeon

Rogue-like

Traditional roguelike game with pixel-art graphics and simple interface.

License: GNU General Public License v3.0 only — Website — Issue Tracker — Source Code — Changelog — Build Metadata

Pixel Dungeon: Enjoy a simpler yet enjoyable roguelike dungeon crawler with pixel art graphics and easy-to-learn controls.

Remember, the best way to discover hidden gems on F-Droid is to explore and try out different games based on your interests. Reading reviews, checking out screenshots, and watching gameplay videos can also guide you towards the perfect game for your next mobile gaming session. Happy gaming! □

Hello, tech beginners! Let's delve into the realm of social media apps on F-Droid. Finding the "best" one depends on what you seek in a social experience. Here are some top contenders in different categories, each catering to specific preferences:

Decentralized & Open-Source Alternatives:

Mastodon

Decentralized social network

Mastodon: Think of it like Twitter, but spread across independent servers, providing greater control and reducing reliance on a single platform.

Privacy-Focused Options:

Nextcloud Dev

Synchronization client

Nextcloud: This self-hosted social media platform gives you complete control over your data and privacy.

Scuttlebutt: If peer-to-peer messaging with a focus on privacy and avoiding centralized servers is your cup of tea, Scuttlebutt is worth exploring.

Friendica

Social networking

The app started as a simple image uploader providing an entry in the "Share"/"Send" menu of Android apps (e.g. the gallery app) to send photos to your Friendica account.

Now it's being extended towards a full interface for Friendica, including timeline display and the ability to view and post on you and your friends' profile walls. You need to have a Friendica account. To get one, choose a site from the Friendica directory. It's free!

License: Mozilla Public License 2.0 — Website — Issue Tracker — Source Code — Build Metadata

Friendica: An open-source social network boasting diverse features for sharing text, photos, videos, and events.

Remember: Each app has its own strengths and weaknesses, so exploring and trying them out based on your interests is key. Consider factors like privacy and data control, the type of content and community you're seeking, your preference for decentralization, and whether the app is user-friendly. Happy exploring in the world of social media! □

Let's explore the world of entertainment apps on F-Droid. Finding the "best" one really hinges on your preferences and the type of entertainment you're after. Here's a lineup of top contenders across different categories that might catch your interest:

Video Streaming:

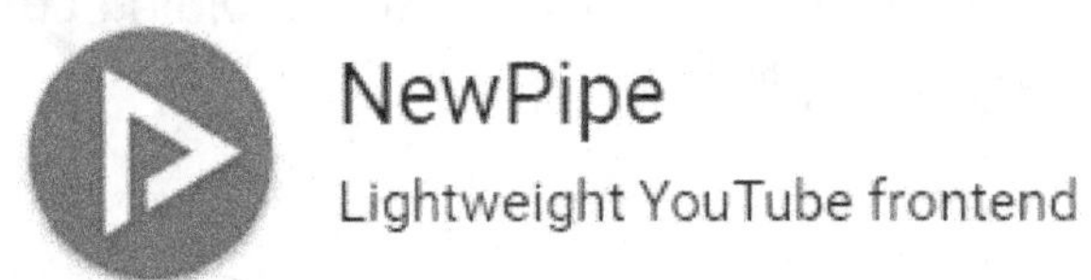

NewPipe

Lightweight YouTube frontend

NewPipe does not use any Google framework libraries, or the YouTube API. It only parses the website in order to gain the information it needs. Therefore this app can be used on devices without Google Services installed. Also, you don't need a YouTube account to use NewPipe, and it's FLOSS.

Anti-Features

This app has features you may not like. Learn more!

 This app promotes or depends entirely on a non-free network service

Author: Team NewPipe — **License:** GNU General Public License v3.0 or later — Website — Issue Tracker — Translation — Source Code — Changelog — Build Metadata

NewPipe: An open-source, ad-free YouTube client that brings features like background playback, audio extraction, and video downloads to the table.

PeerTube: This decentralized video platform offers an alternative to YouTube, emphasizing community-driven content and freedom from censorship.

VLC

The best video and music player. Fast and "just works", plays any file

Video and audio player that supports a wide range of formats, for both local and remote playback.

VLC for Android: A versatile and free media player that can handle almost any video format, be it local files or streamed content.

Music & Podcasts:

*VLC for Android (yes, again!): Besides videos, VLC can cater to your audio needs, playing local music files and podcasts.

AntennaPod

Easy-to-use, flexible and open-source podcast manager and player

AntennaPod: An open-source podcast manager offering features like automatic downloads, playback speed control, and episode queuing.

Funkwhale for Android

The official Android client for Funkwhale

Funkwhale for Android™ is an Android client for Funkwhale, a music streaming server that you can self-host. It uses Funkwhale's native API instead of the subsonic API.

This app requires an account on a Funkwhale instance to work.

You can get support or take a part in Funkwhale's development by visiting our Gitlab project. You can also join us on Matrix.

Source code : https://dev.funkwhale.audio/funkwhale/funkwhale-android
Matrix room: https://matrix.to/#/#funkwhale-android:matrix.org
Funkwhale : https://funkwhale.audio

Author: The Funkwhale Collective — **License:** MIT License — Website — Issue Tracker — Translation — Source Code — Changelog — Build Metadata

Funkwhale: If you're into self-hosted music streaming platforms like SoundCloud, Funkwhale lets you discover and listen to music uploaded by other users.

Reading & News:

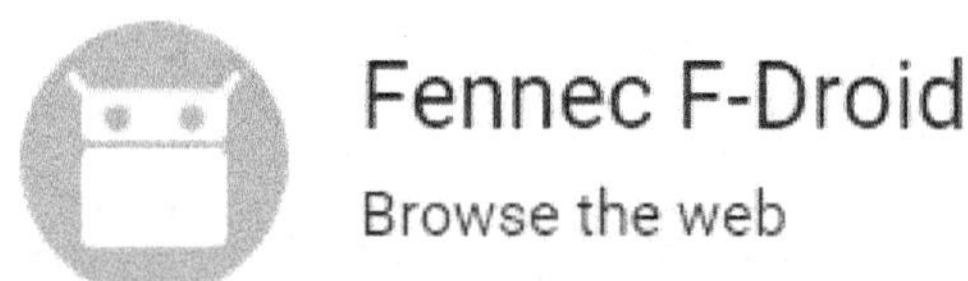

Fennec F-Droid

Browse the web

Browser that supports current and anticipated web standards.

* Improved tracking protection that blocks over 2000 online trackers.
* Private mode available in a single tap.
* Customizable navigation bar position.
* Dark theme.
* Collections of tabs.
* Synchronization across multiple devices.
* Search widget.
* Picture-in-picture mode.

Fennec F-Droid is based on the latest Firefox release (codenamed Fenix).
It has proprietary bits and telemetry removed, but still connects to various Mozilla and Google services that can track users.

Fennec (Firefox fork): An open-source browser with a built-in reader mode, providing a distraction-free reading experience for online articles and webpages.

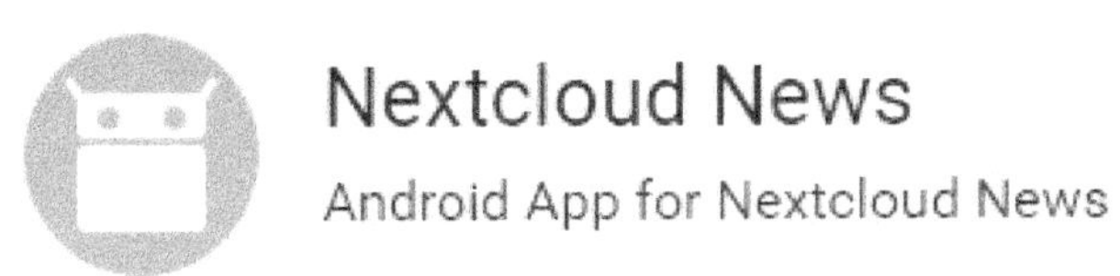

Nextcloud News

Android App for Nextcloud News

The Nextcloud News Reader App makes it possible to synchronize feeds between Android and the Nextcloud News App.

- Dark/Light Theme
- podcast support
- support for Android Auto
- Offline reading
- Cache images offline
- Background synchronization
- Customizable Listview
- Customizable font
- Mark as read while scrolling
- Widget
- and many more!

In order to use the newest beta version, please click on the following link:
https://play.google.com/apps/testing/de.luhmer.owncloudnewsreader

Nextcloud News: Dive into a self-hosted news aggregator that allows you to curate your own news feed from various sources while maintaining control over your data.

Remember, the key to finding your ideal entertainment app is to explore and try out a few based on your interests. Consider factors like the content variety, user-friendliness, and specific features each app offers. Happy exploring in the world of tech entertainment!

Let's navigate the world of communication apps on F-Droid. Figuring out the "best" one depends on your specific needs and preferences. Here's a breakdown of some top contenders in different categories that might suit your fancy:

For general messaging and group chats:

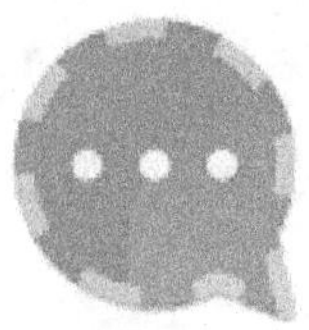

Conversations

Encrypted, easy-to-use XMPP instant messenger for your mobile device

New in version 2.13.0+free

* Easier access to 'Show QR code'
* Support PEP Native Bookmarks
* Add support for SDP Offer / Answer Model (Used by SIP gateways)
* Raise target API to Android 14

Conversations (XMPP): An open-source and versatile app supporting multiple XMPP servers. It offers features like end-to-end encryption, audio/video calls, and file sharing.

SimpleX Chat

SimpleX Chat - e2e encrypted messenger without any user IDs - private by design!

SimpleX - the first messaging platform that has no user identifiers, not even random numbers!
Security assessment was done by Trail of Bits in November 2022.
SimpleX Chat features:

SimpleX Chat: A lightweight and user-friendly app focused on secure messaging. It boasts features like end-to-end encryption, offline messaging, and self-destructing messages.

For decentralized and federated communication:

Element - Secure Messenger

Group messenger - encrypted messaging, group chat and video calls

Element is both a secure messenger and a productivity team collaboration app that is ideal for group chats while remote working. This chat app uses end-to-end encryption to provide powerful video conferencing, file sharing and voice calls.

Element's features include:
- Advanced online communication tools
- Fully encrypted messages to allow safer corporate communication, even for remote workers
- Decentralized chat based on the Matrix open source framework
- File sharing securely with encrypted data while managing projects
- Video chats with Voice over IP and screen sharing
- Easy integration with your favourite online collaboration tools, project management tools, VoIP services and other team messaging apps

Matrix: An open-source and decentralized communication protocol that allows connection across different servers and platforms. Apps like Element provide user-friendly interfaces for Matrix communication.

Briar

Secure Messaging, Anywhere

Briar is a messaging app designed for activists, journalists, and anyone else who needs a safe, easy and robust way to communicate. Unlike traditional messaging tools such as email, Twitter or Telegram, Briar doesn't rely on a central server - messages are synchronized directly between the users' devices. If the Internet's down, Briar can sync via Bluetooth or Wi-Fi, keeping the information flowing in a crisis. If the Internet's up, Briar can sync via the Tor network, protecting users and their relationships from surveillance.

Briar: A secure and offline-first messaging app utilizing Bluetooth and Wi-Fi direct for local communication, making it ideal for areas with limited internet access.

Manyverse

A social network off the grid

Manyverse is a social network app using the SSB protocol (Secure Scuttlebutt) where you can write posts and share with friends nearby or over the internet. It's different from mainstream social networks because your data is yours, it lives on your phone, not in the cloud. So there is no login, no company holding your data, no ads, no tracking of your activity, it's just you and your friends! The app is free and open source software, and it will always remain free.

Features:

* Write threads of posts (even when offline) and share them with friends (over the internet or nearby via Wi-Fi or Bluetooth)
* Private chats
* Emoji reactions
* Profile pages with biographies
* Attach pictures, add content warnings
* More features as we develop the app!

Scuttlebutt: A peer-to-peer messaging app with a focus on privacy and avoiding reliance on centralized servers.

For niche communities and interests:

Mobilizon

Mobilizon is a tool to help manage your events, your profiles and your groups.

New in version 1.0.2

- Cache not cleared when a new release is available
- New localizations

Mobilizon: An event management platform designed for organizing and joining offline events within specific communities.

Jami

Audio & Video Calls / Chat Take Control of your Communication!

Jami (a GNU package) is a universal and distributed communication platform which respects the freedoms and privacy of users.
It is 100% Free software. Available on all platforms.

★ Communicate freely with Jami:
- send text messages
- make audio calls
- make video calls
- share pictures and files

★ Reach your peers directly in peer to peer !

★ Use your Jami account on multiple devices !

★ Available on Windows, macOS, iOS, GNU/Linux, Android and Android TV !

★ SIP account support available !

★ Next additions: audio/video call recording (Android), group chat...

Jami: An open-source audio/video calling app offering end-to-end encryption and support for both one-on-one and group calls.

Remember: Consider factors like the type of communication you need (text, voice, video), privacy and security features, and the communities or people you want to connect with when choosing an app. Don't hesitate to try out different options and see what works best for you! Happy communicating! □□

Let's navigate the world of everyday tasks and productivity apps on F-Droid. Finding the best ones depends on your specific needs and preferences, but here's a collection of top contenders across different categories to make your exploration easier:

To-Do Lists and Task Management:

Super Productivity

Free to do list & time tracker for programmers & designers

New in version 21.0

- Fix webdav sync issue

Organize your daily tasks at one place while making time tracking a lot less annoying. Super Productivity is a ToDo List / Time Tracker / Personal Jira Task Manager for multiple platforms.

- *Super Productivity:* An open-source and feature-rich to-do list app with time tracking, calendar integration, and progress reports.

Notes and Organization:

Joplin

a note taking and to-do app with sync between Linux, macOS, Windows, and mobile

Note: This release can lag significantly behind the official release which can be an issue when a timely update is needed. It may be less secure because the app might have a known security vulnerability for several days, even if the official app has been patched. It does not have camera capabilities. Issues with this version might be raised on https://gitlab.com/fdroid/fdroiddata for user @muelli

- *Joplin:* An open-source and cross-platform note-taking app with encryption, markdown formatting, and automatic syncing.

Calendars and Scheduling:

Simple Calendar Pro

Calendar widget 2023. Appointment scheduler & planner. Business work calendar

New in version 6.23.1

* Fixed a yearly view display issue
* Allow starting the week with any day
* Added some translation, stability and UX improvements

- *Simple Calendar Pro:* A highly customizable and offline calendar app with an agenda planner, event reminders, and various calendar views.

Month Calendar Widget

Calendar widget

Simple month calendar widget.

License: Apache License 2.0 — Issue Tracker — Source Code — Build Metadata

- *Month:* A minimalist and beautiful calendar app with a focus on simplicity and clear visualization of your schedule.

Time Management and Focus:

TimeLimit.io

Flexibly limit the usage duration

New in version 6.18.0

- fix issue with the self limitation adding
- update contained components

- *TimeLimit.io:* A flexible timer app to limit your usage of specific apps or websites, helping you control your digital habits.

Bonus:

Simple File Manager Pro

Handy file explorer for easily searching or organizing your files and folders

New in version 6.16.1

* Added SD card to storage analysis
* Added some UI, translation and stability improvements

- *Simple File Manager:* A lightweight and user-friendly file manager with essential features for keeping your files organized.

New in version 6.603

- Fixed settings import/export of identities without a name or description

K-9 Mail is an open source email client that works with basically every email provider.

- *K-9 Mail:* A secure and open-source email client for managing your email efficiently.

Remember: This is just a small selection, and F-Droid offers a vast library of everyday tasks and productivity apps. Explore the "Productivity" and "Tools" categories within the app, and don't hesitate to try out different options based on your needs and preferences. Happy exploring!

Let's explore the world of security and privacy apps on F-Droid. Determining the "best" options depends on your specific threats and goals, but here's a list of top contenders across different categories to help you prioritize and dive into:

General Security:

Aegis Authenticator

Free, secure and open source 2FA app to manage tokens for your online services

Aegis Authenticator is a free, secure and open source app to manage your 2-step verification tokens for your online services.

- *Aegis Authenticator:* An open-source two-factor authentication (2FA) app that supports multiple accounts, providing an extra layer of security for logins.

NetGuard

A simple way to block access to the internet per application

NetGuard provides simple and advanced ways to block access to the internet - no root required.

Applications and addresses can individually be allowed or denied access to your Wi-Fi and/or mobile connection.

Blocking access to the internet can help:

* reduce your data usage
* save your battery
* increase your privacy

- *NetGuard:* A customizable firewall app that controls internet access for individual apps and blocks unwanted connections, improving network security.

OpenKeychain: Easy PGP

Encrypt your Files and Communications. Compatible with the OpenPGP Standard.

- *OpenKeychain:* An open-source and secure password manager with offline storage and encryption, ensuring the protection of your login credentials.

Privacy-Focused Browsing:

DuckDuckGo Privacy Browser

Privacy, simplified

New in version 5.181.1

Squashed some bugs that were running around.

Join our fully distributed team and help raise the standard of trust online — from anywhere! https://duckduckgo.com/hiring

- *DuckDuckGo Privacy Browser:* A search engine and browser prioritizing privacy with built-in trackers and ad blockers.

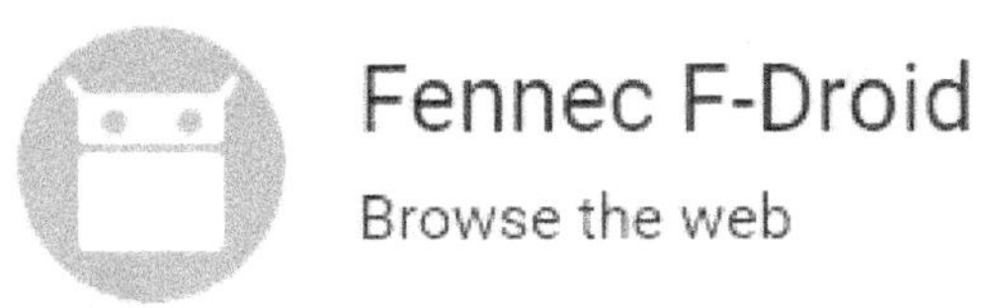

Fennec F-Droid

Browse the web

Browser that supports current and anticipated web standards.

* Improved tracking protection that blocks over 2000 online trackers.
* Private mode available in a single tap.
* Customizable navigation bar position.
* Dark theme.
* Collections of tabs.
* Synchronization across multiple devices.
* Search widget.
* Picture-in-picture mode.

- *Fennec (Firefox fork):* An open-source browser with various privacy and customization features, such as blocking scripts and fingerprinting.

Remember: The effectiveness of these apps depends on your specific threat model and the practices you combine them with. Consider factors like your level of technical expertise, the threats you face (such as online tracking, data breaches, or government surveillance), and your budget. Most F-Droid apps are free, but some may offer premium features or require paid services like VPNs. Happy exploring!

Let's dive into the world of lifestyle apps on F-Droid. Finding the "best" ones is subjective, but here are some top contenders across different categories to cater to your diverse needs:

Food and Nutrition:

OpenFoodFacts

Look up food ingredients, allergens, nutrition facts

Scan food products or their barcode to obtain data on ingredients, additives,
allergens, nutrition facts…
The app allows to view the 1.500.000 products already contained in the free and open
database Open Food Facts.
More importantly, it also lets you easily be part of the solution:
* contribute pictures and data for missing products
* team up with the Open Food Facts Artificial Intelligence by answering its blue questions

- *Open Food Facts*: Scan barcodes, check food ingredients and nutritional
  information, and make informed dietary choices.

Finance and Budgeting:

MoneyWallet

Expense Manager

MoneyWallet is an advanced expense manager that allows you to track your expenses and plan budgets. You can organize your data using custom categories, events, places and people tags. The user interface is in material design, clear, simple and extremely customizable. It fits on all devices. It's simply your best expense manager.

License: GNU General Public License v3.0 only — Issue Tracker — Source Code — Changelog — Build Metadata

- *MoneyWallet:* Track your income and expenses, categorize transactions, and manage your budget effectively.

Bonus:

OpenTracks

A sport tracker buddy that respects your privacy.

New in version v4.10.1

v4.10.1: OpenTracks

Changes:
- Android 14: crash on recording start if permissions are not granted
- Chart titles are more compact

- *OpenTracks:* An open-source sleep tracker to understand your sleep patterns and improve sleep quality.

Remember: This is just a glimpse into the diverse world of Lifestyle apps on F-Droid. Explore the "Health," "Finance," "Productivity," and "Tools" categories to discover more hidden gems tailored to your specific needs and preferences. Don't hesitate to try out different apps and find the perfect tools to enhance your overall well-being and live a fulfilling life! □

Let's delve into the world of education apps on F-Droid. Discovering the "best" ones depends on your learning goals and interests, but here's a list of top contenders across different categories to guide your exploration:

Formal Education and Language Learning:

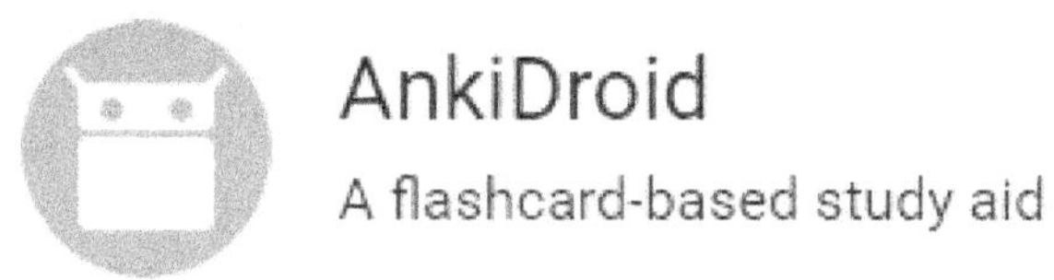

AnkiDroid

A flashcard-based study aid

Anki is a program which makes remembering things easy. Because it is a lot more efficient than traditional study methods, you can either greatly decrease your time spent studying, or greatly increase the amount you learn. AnkiDroid is the Android port of Anki, and is compatible with Anki data.

Opt-in synchronization uses the non-free AnkiWeb service by default, but this can be changed in the settings to use, for example, an instance of the unofficial Anki Sync Server).

- *AnkiDroid:* A flashcard app with spaced repetition algorithms for effective memorization of vocabulary, facts, and concepts.

Jitsi Meet

Instant video conferences efficiently adapting to your scale

Jitsi Meet lets you stay in touch with all your teams, be they family, friends, or colleagues. Instant video conferences, efficiently adapting to your scale.

- *Jitsi Meet:* A secure and open-source video conferencing platform for online classes and group study sessions.

STEM Education and Practical Skills:

phyphox

Perform physics experiments with your phone. (by the RWTH Aachen University)

Did you know that you are carrying a 3D magnetometer? That you can use your phone as a pendulum to measure earth\'s local gravitational acceleration? That you can turn your phone into a sonar?

- *Phyphox:* A science lab in your pocket, connecting your phone's sensors to explore physics, chemistry, and other scientific concepts through experiments.

VLC

The best video and music player. Fast and "just works", plays any file

Video and audio player that supports a wide range of formats, for both local and remote playback.

- *VLC for Android:* A powerful media player for playing educational videos, documentaries, and lectures.

Let's explore how F-Droid can help you manage your finances with its focus on open-source and privacy-oriented apps. Here are some excellent options across different categories:

Budgeting and Expense Tracking:

My Expenses

Easy to use personal finance manager: rich functionality and Open Source

New in version 3.7.1.1

Bug fixes

https://github.com/mtotschnig/MyExpenses/projects/123#column-19716731

- *My Expenses:* An easy-to-use and feature-rich app for recording income and expenses, categorizing transactions, and generating reports.

OpenMoneyBox

Budget management application

New in version 3.4.2.6

Changelog v3.4.2.6:
- Added splash screen colors;
- Removed unused permissions (Phone and Network status);
- compileSdk 34;
- AndroidChart v3.1.0.18;
- osmdroid 6.1.17.

- *OpenMoneyBox:* An open-source budget management application with envelope budgeting and goal tracking features.

Sushi - Personal Finance

Keep track of your own finances

New in version 1.15

- Global filters
- New theme "Wasabi"

- *Sushi - Personal Finance:* An open-source app with multi-wallet support, transaction tagging, and income/expense analysis tools.

Investment and Portfolio Management:

CoinTrend: Private Crypto Tracker

Lightweight, fast and private cryptocurrencies monitor

New in version 1.3.1

New features:
- Settings: set the tracking configuration you need for your cryptocurrencies. The price change percentage shown in the coins' lists can now be set to track several different time frames, even the larger ones.
- About: check all the CoinTrend's information in one place: quickly access the source code repository and the changelog one click away; request new features and improvements directly from your smartphone through our email or by opening a detailed GitHub Issue; support the de

- *Crypto Tracker:* A lightweight and private app for tracking cryptocurrency prices and managing your portfolio.

Remember: F-Droid provides a variety of tools to help you take control of your finances while prioritizing privacy. Explore these categories, try out different apps, and find the perfect ones to keep your financial matters in check! □□

Let's explore some travel apps on F-Droid to enhance your journey. The "best" ones depend on your travel style, so here are top contenders in different categories to help you plan and enjoy your adventures:

Maps and Navigation:

OsmAnd~

Global Mobile Map Viewing & Navigation for Offline and Online OSM Maps

OsmAnd+ (OSM Automated Navigation Directions) is a map and navigation application with access to the free, worldwide, and high-quality OpenStreetMap (OSM) data.
Enjoy voice and optical navigation, viewing POIs (points of interest), creating and managing GPX tracks, using contour lines visualization and altitude info, a choice between driving, cycling, pedestrian modes, OSM editing and much more.

- *OsmAnd+:* An open-source offline maps and navigation app with features like hiking and cycling routes, public transport information, and points of interest.

Organic Maps: Hike, Bike, Drive Offline

Navigate with Privacy - Community-Driven & Open-Source

New in version 2023.12.20-4-FDroid

Christmas & New Year gifts for you from Organic Maps community:
• Outdoors map style for hiking, cycling, and exploring the Nature
• Search for village addresses without streets in Austria, Czechia, Germany, Poland, Slovakia
• Type "skiing" to find downhill & Nordic pistes
• OpenStreetMap map data as of December 13
• Check photos, reviews, and prices for some hotels. All your donations and bookings contribute to the development of Organic Maps!

- *Organic Maps:* Another open-source offline maps and navigation app with a focus on privacy and community-driven data.

Transportation and Planning:

Transportr - Public Transit

Free Public Transport Assistant without Ads or Tracking

New in version 2.2.0

* Switch map library to MapLibre - finally bringing Transportr back to F-Droid!
* Remember preferred means of transport for future searches (thanks Prat!)
* Fix minor issues on About page and with the time picker (thanks Altonss!)
* Fix and re-add formerly broken regions: SBB (thanks Tobias!), VVO, AVV (Augsburg), GVH, VRS
* Remove regions where information is no longer available: VOR, STV, VVV, SNCB, 9292, TFI
* Remove a long list of regions that are no longer served by Navitia

- *Transit:* Access public transport information and plan trips for many cities worldwide.

Language and Communication:

OpenKeychain: Easy PGP

Encrypt your Files and Communications. Compatible with the OpenPGP Standard.

- *OpenKeychain:* An open-source and secure password manager to keep your login credentials safe on the go.

Remember: F-Droid offers various apps catering to different travel needs. Explore these categories, try out different apps, and find the ones that make your travels smoother and more enjoyable! ✈ □□□